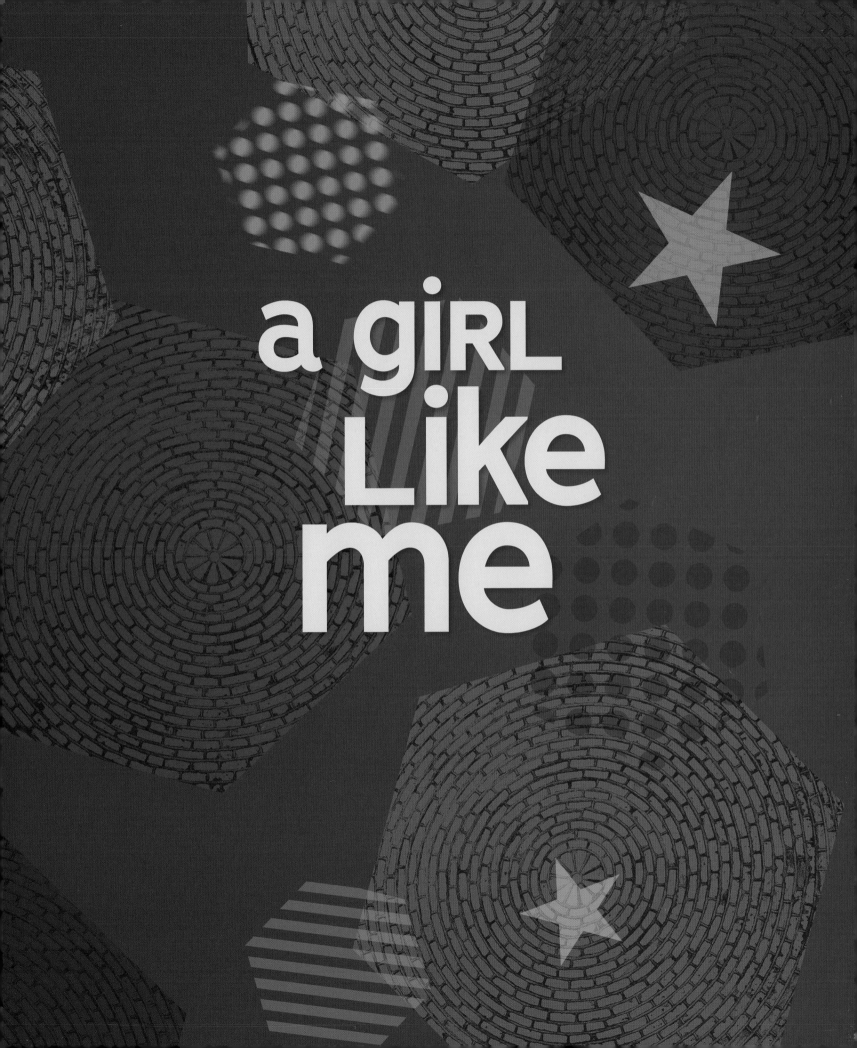

a girl
like
me

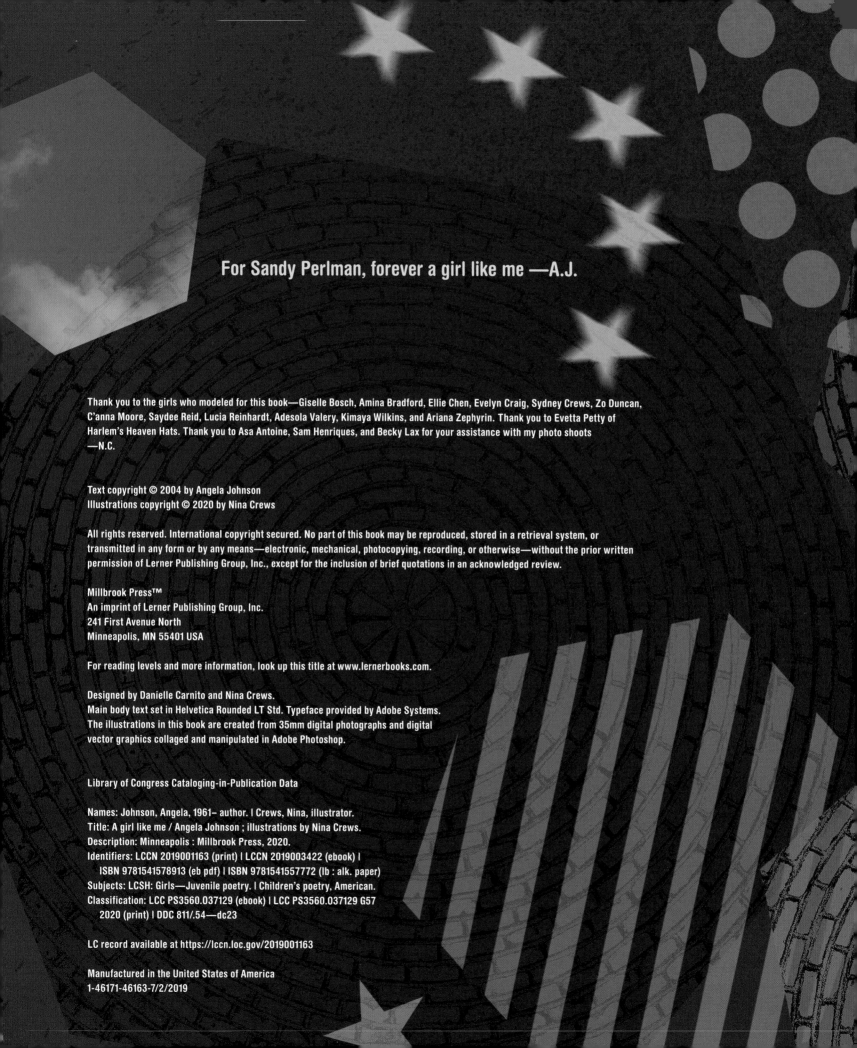

For Sandy Perlman, forever a girl like me —A.J.

Thank you to the girls who modeled for this book—Giselle Bosch, Amina Bradford, Ellie Chen, Evelyn Craig, Sydney Crews, Zo Duncan, C'anna Moore, Saydee Reid, Lucia Reinhardt, Adesola Valery, Kimaya Wilkins, and Ariana Zephyrin. Thank you to Evetta Petty of Harlem's Heaven Hats. Thank you to Asa Antoine, Sam Henriques, and Becky Lax for your assistance with my photo shoots —N.C.

Millbrook Press™
An imprint of Lerner Publishing Group, Inc.
241 First Avenue North
Minneapolis, MN 55401 USA

For reading levels and more information, look up this title at www.lernerbooks.com.

Designed by Danielle Carnito and Nina Crews.
Main body text set in Helvetica Rounded LT Std. Typeface provided by Adobe Systems.
The illustrations in this book are created from 35mm digital photographs and digital vector graphics collaged and manipulated in Adobe Photoshop.

Library of Congress Cataloging-in-Publication Data

Names: Johnson, Angela, 1961– author. | Crews, Nina, illustrator.
Title: A girl like me / Angela Johnson ; illustrations by Nina Crews.
Description: Minneapolis : Millbrook Press, 2020.
Identifiers: LCCN 2019001163 (print) | LCCN 2019003422 (ebook) |
    ISBN 9781541578913 (eb pdf) | ISBN 9781541557772 (lb : alk. paper)
Subjects: LCSH: Girls—Juvenile poetry. | Children's poetry, American.
Classification: LCC PS3560.037129 (ebook) | LCC PS3560.037129 G57
    2020 (print) | DDC 811/.54—dc23

LC record available at https://lccn.loc.gov/2019001163

Manufactured in the United States of America
1-46171-46163-7/2/2019

a girl Like me

Angela Johnson

illustrations by Nina Crews

M
Millbrook Press
Minneapolis

I always dream

I'm flying
in Supergirl
underwear
way
up
high,

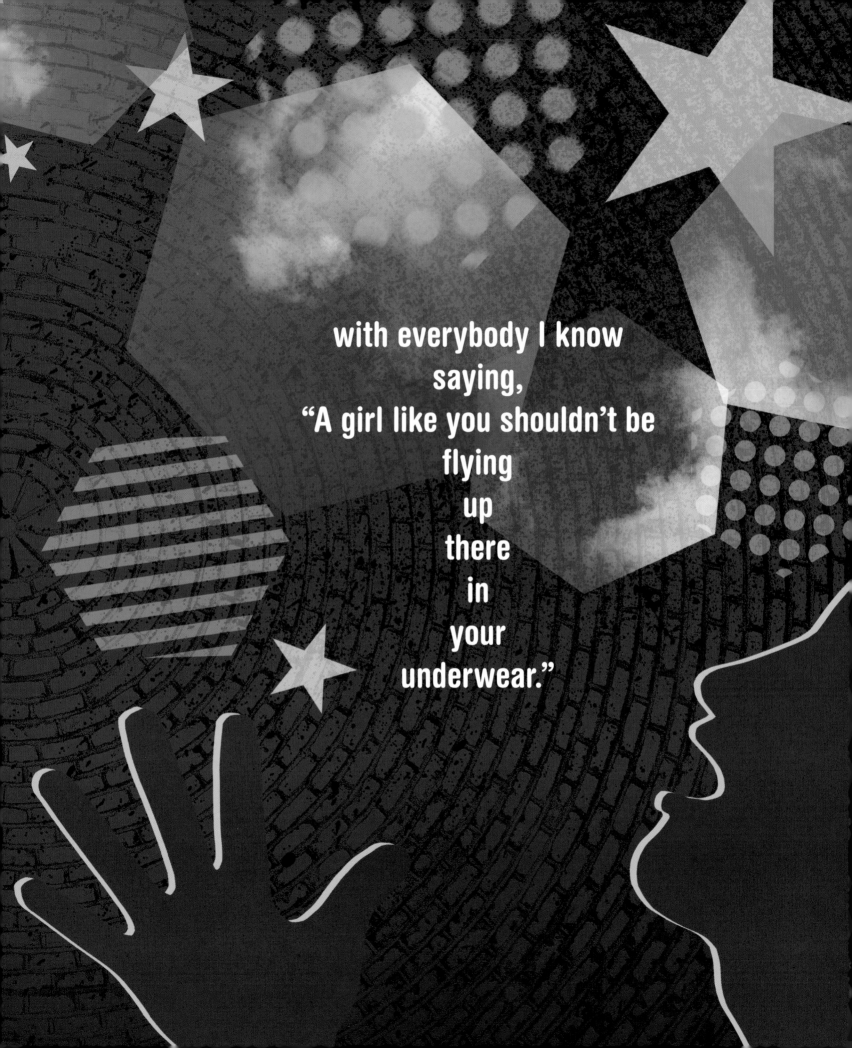

with everybody I know
saying,
"A girl like you shouldn't be
flying
up
there
in
your
underwear."

I used to dream
I walked over tall buildings
in flowing scarves and a cowgirl hat.

Never was scared or paid
attention when people
I knew said, "A girl like you needs to stop
walking over those tall buildings
in funny clothes and
get down here with
the rest of us."

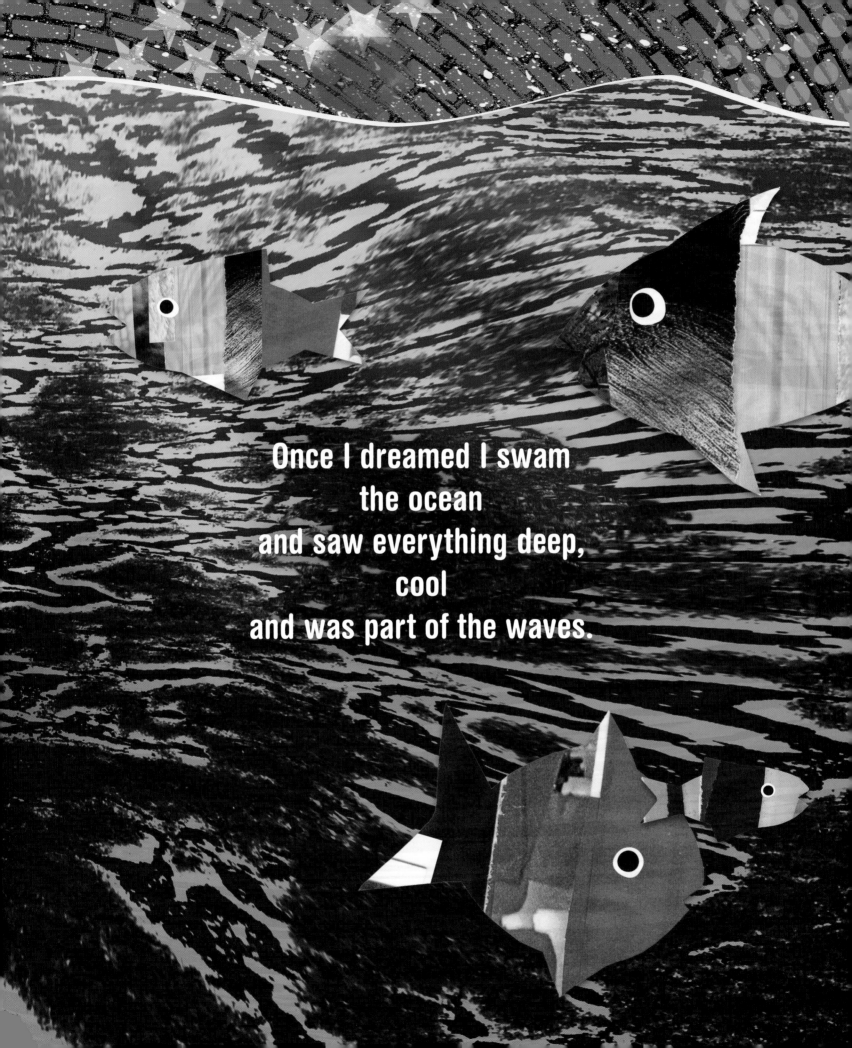

Once I dreamed I swam
the ocean
and saw everything deep,
cool
and was part of the waves.

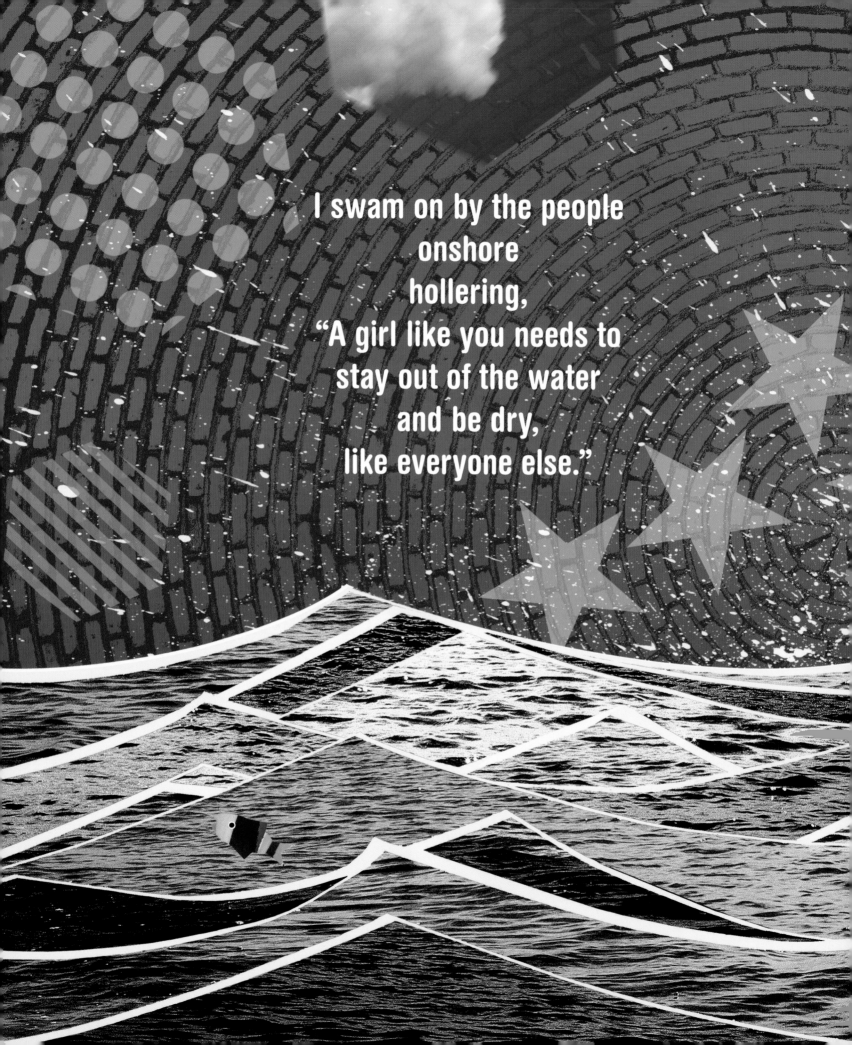

I swam on by the people
onshore
hollering,
"A girl like you needs to
stay out of the water
and be dry,
like everyone else."

So . . .
Yesterday

I bought
a cape and more hats,

borrowed some scarves
from my mom,

and walked past
tall buildings

to the ocean

'cause a girl like me
should always be
thinking
way up
high

and making
everything
better than
the dream.

a giRL Like me:

My favorite color is pink. I would like to make my community a better place. I want to be a lawyer when I grow up.

I am a girl that loves my friends. I would like to travel to Japan and Belize. When I grow up, I want to be an actress and travel all over the world.

I am funny, kind, smart, musical, and brave. If I were an inventor, I would create shoes that could turn into roller skates, ice skates, or springs.

I like swimming, dancing, singing, food, sports, and toys. I also loooove color! My wish for the world is that no one is treated unfairly again.

My favorite anything is gymnastics. I love my family. I wish that everyone can be the best that they can be. I am humbled, funny, and loved.

My favorite anythings are unicorns and making friends. If I were an inventor, I would create a teleporter. I wish to be successful.

My favorite food is pizza. My favorite color is pink. I am outgoing, adventurous, and smart. When I grow up, I want to be an actor.

My favorite color is purple. I am very funny and like to just dance around the room and have fun. My wish for the world is to be nice to other people and treat them with respect.

If I were an inventor, I would invent a portal that leads to a land filled with puppies and cotton candy. I want to be a veterinarian when I grow up.

I am sassy, funny, and kind. I wish for the world to stop littering. When I grow up, I want to be an inventor.

My favorite colors are pink and baby blue. I am a vegan! Which means I do not eat anything that is an animal product.

My favorite color is yellow. I am an artist. I am very passionate about making art available to everyone, including on buildings and streets.

WHO ARE YOU?